Inside My Body

Why do I have periods?

Isabel Thomas

 Raintree

www.raintreepublishers.co.uk
Visit our website to find out more information about Raintree books.

To order:
☎ Phone 0845 6044371
🖷 Fax +44 (0) 1865 312263
🖳 Email myorders@raintreepublishers.co.uk

Customers from outside the UK please telephone +44 1865 312262

Raintree is an imprint of Capstone Global Library Limited, a company incorporated in England and Wales having its registered office at 7 Pilgrim Street, London, EC4V 6LB – Registered company number: 6695582

Edited by Kate de Villiers and Laura Knowles
Designed by Steve Mead
Illustrations by KJA-artists.com
Picture research by Mica Brancic
Originated by Capstone Global Library Ltd
Printed and bound in China by CTPS

ISBN 978 1 406 22104 6 (hardback)
15 14 13 12 11
10 9 8 7 6 5 4 3 2 1

British Library Cataloguing in Publication Data
Thomas, Isabel
Why do I have periods?. -- (Inside my body)
612.6'62-dc22
A full catalogue record for this book is available from the British Library.

Acknowledgements
We would like to thank the following for permission to reproduce photographs: Getty Images pp. **5** (Photodisc/Ebby May), **9** (Brand X Pictures/Eric Raptosh Photography), **11** (Iconica/John Giustina), **17** (Digital Vision/Tom Le Goff), **23** (Stockbyte), **26** (Blend Images/ Priscilla Gragg), **28** (Mark Andersen), **29** (Rubberball); iStockphoto.com pp. **6** (© Jodi Jacobson), **7** (© Robert Churchill), **25** (© Nancy Catherine Walker); Science Photo Library pp. **8** (Scott Camazine), **13** (Professors P M Motta & J Van Blerkom), **27** (Lemoine), **19** (Neil Bromhall), **15** (Scott Camazine).

Photographic design details reproduced with permission of Shutterstock pp. **7**, **12**, **16**, **24** (© Isaac Marzioli), **7**, **12**, **16**, **24** (© Yurok).

Cover photograph of girl holding her painful abdomen reproduced with permission of Science Photo Library/ A J Photo.

We would like to thank David Wright for his invaluable help in the preparation of this book.

Every effort has been made to contact copyright holders of any material reproduced in this book. Any omissions will be rectified in subsequent printings if notice is given to the publisher.

All the Internet addresses (URLs) given in this book were valid at the time of going to press. However, due to the dynamic nature of the Internet, some addresses may have changed, or sites may have changed or ceased to exist since publication. While the author and publisher regret any inconvenience this may cause readers, no responsibility for any such changes can be accepted by either the author or the publisher.

Contents

Words that appear in the text in bold, **like this**, are explained in the glossary on page 30.

What is a period?

Like all animals, humans change as they grow older. Think about the people in your family. Children are very different from babies. Adults are very different from children. Both our bodies and brains develop and **mature** over time. It's also easy to spot differences between boys and girls. Their bodies mature in different ways as they grow up.

Changing bodies

One of the biggest changes for a girl comes with her first period. This is a sign that amazing new things are happening inside her body. It's an important step towards becoming an adult woman.

A girl's periods start during a time of growth and change called **puberty**. Boys also go through puberty, but they don't get periods. Their bodies change in different ways.

Extreme body fact

How many periods will I have?
The average girl starts having periods when she is 12, and has one every month (except when she is pregnant) until she is around 50 years old. This adds up to around 450 periods in a lifetime.

It's good to talk things over with your friends. Remember that everyone is different. Some of your friends will start puberty earlier than you, and some will start later.

Why do I need to go through puberty?

All living things reproduce themselves to make new individuals. Humans reproduce by having babies. This process is called **reproduction** and it is part of our life **cycle**. **Puberty** prepares our bodies for reproduction when we are adults.

🔍 Some mammals, such as this dog, have several babies at a time. Most humans have one baby at a time.

Mammal life

Humans are mammals. This means that, as in other mammals, a new baby grows inside the mother's body. The baby grows in a special organ called the **uterus**, also known as the womb. After the baby is born, the mother's body produces milk to feed the baby.

Men and women have different roles in reproduction. A woman's body makes special **cells** called **egg cells**. Her uterus supports a growing baby, and her breasts produce milk. A man's body makes **sperm cells**. The changes that happen during puberty prepare our bodies for these roles.

Practical advice

Where can I find out the truth about puberty?

Puberty is a normal, natural process, but some people find it difficult and embarrassing to talk about. Other people might make things up to fill in the gaps in what they know. Don't believe everything your friends tell you about puberty. The best source of information is a parent or carer, teacher, or a library book like this one.

How does puberty start?

Puberty can begin any time between the ages of 8 and 18. The average age is 11 for girls and 13 for boys, which means that roughly half of your friends will start before this age, and half will start afterwards.

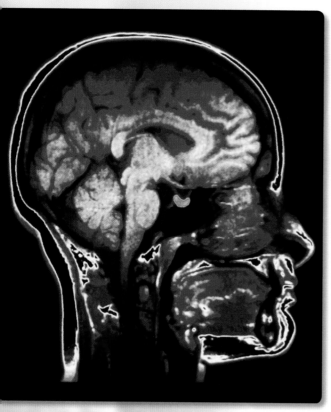

Your brain is your body's control centre. A tiny area called the pituitary gland (shown here in green) makes the hormones that start puberty off.

Puberty starts when your brain releases special **hormones** into your blood. These messenger chemicals travel through your body, carrying the news that it's time to develop and **mature**.

Sex hormones

Your body begins to make new hormones, called sex hormones. They are different depending on whether you are a boy or a girl.

The sex hormones make your whole body grow more quickly. Both boys and girls grow taller during puberty. This is called a **growth spurt**.

My friends have all started their periods, so I know what to expect.

I got my first period when I was 10.

As the messages that start puberty come from deep inside your brain, you can't do anything to change the timing. Try not to compare yourself to friends. The timing will be perfect for your body.

How will my body change?

When **puberty** begins, **hormones** start to cause changes. You can see some of these changes from the outside. Others take place inside the body and you won't even notice them.

Both boys and girls grow taller during puberty. Other changes take place only in boys or only in girls.

SCIENCE BEHIND THE MYTH

MYTH: All teenage girls wear bras.

SCIENCE: Girls begin wearing bras at different times. Bras help to support growing breasts and make you feel comfortable. You can start wearing one whenever you feel ready, but make sure that it fits well. A relative or friend can help you to shop for a bra. Some shops have fitters who can help you to find one that is perfect for your body. Remember to get fitted for a new bra as your breasts grow.

Growing breasts is one of the first signs of puberty in girls. Your nipples may get darker and stick out more. You may feel small bumps behind them. Your breasts will gradually get bigger and softer as hormones tell your body to store fat there. Don't worry if your breasts seem to develop slowly or even at different speeds – it can take up to four years before they finish growing.

Hormones also make your body hairier, especially under your arms and between your legs. This is called pubic hair. At the same time, your body gets curvier as your hip bones widen, and fat is stored on your hips, thighs, and bottom.

Puberty can mean fun shopping trips to find new clothes for your growing body.

Why do girls get periods?

After **puberty** begins and a girl's breasts start to develop, her body gets ready for her first period.

A period is the name given to monthly bleeding from the **vagina**. This is not bleeding like when you cut your finger. It is carefully controlled by your body, and completely healthy. It is a sign that a special **cycle** is taking place inside your body.

Practical advice

When should I expect to get my first period?

A girl's first period often starts about two years after her breasts start developing. This is thought to be when her body reaches a certain weight. Before your periods start, you might notice a thin, white liquid in your knickers – this is completely normal.

Changes inside your body

The cycle involves your **uterus** (womb) and **ovaries**. Your uterus is a pear-shaped organ that sits just above your bladder. You have two ovaries, one on each side of your uterus. Each ovary is about the size and shape of a walnut.

The **hormones** that rush around your body at puberty make these organs do new things. During childhood, the ovaries grow. At puberty, they begin to release special **cells** called eggs. A girl starts to have periods when her ovaries begin to produce **egg cells**.

This image shows an egg being released from an ovary.

Why do periods come every month?

Every month a woman's body goes through a process called the **menstrual cycle**. It is named after an old word for "month" because it takes around 28 days from start to finish.

🔍 The menstrual cycle involves several different organs inside a girl's body.

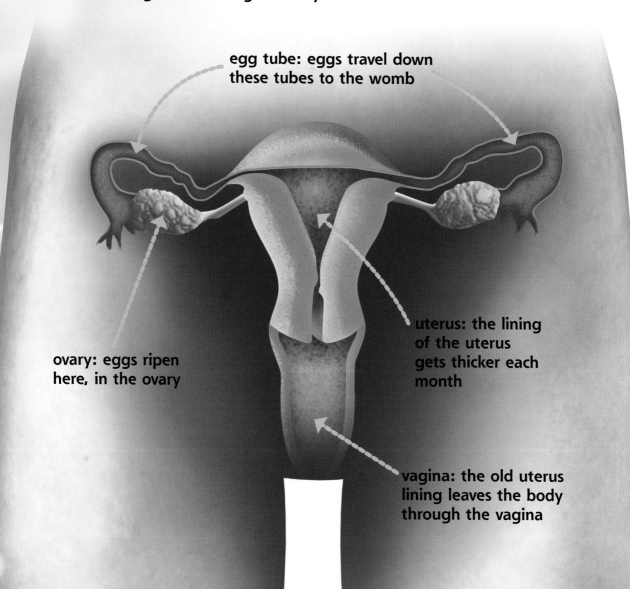

egg tube: eggs travel down these tubes to the womb

uterus: the lining of the uterus gets thicker each month

ovary: eggs ripen here, in the ovary

vagina: the old uterus lining leaves the body through the vagina

Once a month, **hormones** cause an **ovary** to release one ripe egg. This egg travels down a special tube towards the **uterus**. Its journey takes four to seven days.

At the same time, hormones prepare the womb in case the egg is **fertilized** and starts to grow into a baby. The uterus lining becomes at least five times thicker. Lots of blood starts to flow through the lining, ready to bring nutrients to a growing baby.

An egg can only be fertilized by a **sperm cell** (see page 18). This means that most eggs arrive at the womb without being fertilized. The lining of the womb starts to break down so that a brand new lining can build up next month. The old egg, blood, and womb lining leave your body through the **vagina**. This is your period.

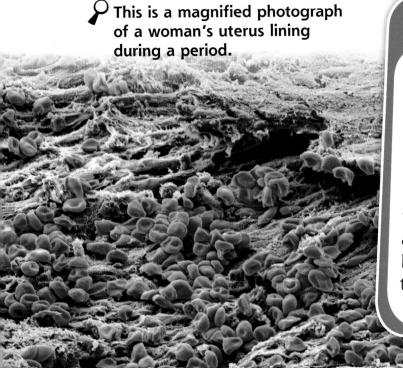

This is a magnified photograph of a woman's uterus lining during a period.

Extreme body fact

How much blood comes out during a period?
The average girl loses two to three tablespoons of blood during a period, but it's normal to lose as much as four-fifths of a cup full, or as little as three teaspoons. Bleeding usually lasts for three to five days.

What is it like to have a period?

At first, your periods might not come every month. Gradually, your body will settle into a routine.

Many girls and women start to notice that they feel different for a few days before their period starts. Some feel tired, snappy, or sad. Others feel a little sick or get headaches. Some women find they get sore breasts, and a bloated, sticking-out tummy.

These feelings are caused by the **hormones** racing around your body. They even have their own name: pre-menstrual syndrome (PMS).

Practical advice

Period pain

When a period comes, some women feel cramps or pains in their lower belly. This is called period pain and doctors think it may be caused by the muscles in the womb wall gently squeezing the old lining out of the body. Resting with a hot water bottle or heating pad on your stomach can help to soothe period cramps and backache.

🔍 Resting with a hot water bottle on your stomach can help to soothe period cramps and backache.

Should I use tampons or sanitary towels?

There are several different ways to catch the blood that comes out during a period. Many girls like to start with sanitary towels. You can keep one in your bag ready for when your period starts. Keep it clean and safe inside a pocket or tin. Once your periods start, you can practise using tampons. These are designed to sit inside your **vagina** and soak up the blood before it comes out. Every pack comes with instructions but it's important to only practise using them when you are actually bleeding.

What is pregnancy?

Egg cells and **sperm cells** each contain half the information needed to make a baby. Fertilization is when one sperm cell (from the father) joins together with one egg cell inside the mother's body. The **fertilized** egg contains all the information needed to make a baby.

The fertilized egg buries itself in the **uterus** lining, which is full of blood and nutrients. The egg cell copies itself over and over again. This makes new **cells** that develop into different parts of the baby's body.

It takes nine months for a tiny fertilized egg, just a tenth of a millimetre across, to develop into a baby. After eight weeks, the growing baby is just the size of a grape but most of its main body parts have already formed. One cell has become almost one billion cells.

Extreme body facts

How many eggs?
A baby girl is born with a lifetime's supply of egg cells in her **ovaries**. About 450 eggs are released before her periods stop. A woman releases one egg cell every month, but a man's **testicles** can make thousands of sperm cells every second!

The growing baby is called a foetus. At 20 weeks, this foetus weighs about 500 grams (18 ounces).

The baby is surrounded by a special liquid, which helps to control the baby's temperature and protect it.

This cord brings blood full of food and oxygen to the baby.

🔍 This photograph shows a baby inside its mother's uterus.

Why don't boys have periods?

Periods are part of a **cycle** that prepares a woman's body to carry a baby. A boy's body changes in different ways as he grows into a man.

Changes during puberty

Boys are born with two **testicles** instead of **ovaries**. They sit inside a bag of skin. During **puberty**, the testicles start to make **sperm cells**. They also produce male sex **hormones**, which cause other body changes.

SCIENCE BEHIND THE MYTH

MYTH: Boys are taller than girls.

SCIENCE: For a while, girls are often taller than boys. Most boys start their **growth spurt** towards the end of puberty, two or more years later than most girls. Before their growth spurts, boys will be shorter, but they soon catch up and overtake girls.

As a boy goes through puberty, new body hair appears under his arms, between his legs, and on his face and chest. The boy's voice "breaks" and becomes deeper as his voice box grows. Hormones make his heart and other muscles grow. He becomes fitter and stronger, with wider shoulders.

A boy's testicles and **penis** also grow and develop. His testicles begin to produce sperm cells. His body begins to produce fluids that mix with the sperm cells and provide them with energy. The mixture of sperm cells and fluid is called semen. It leaves the boy's body through his penis.

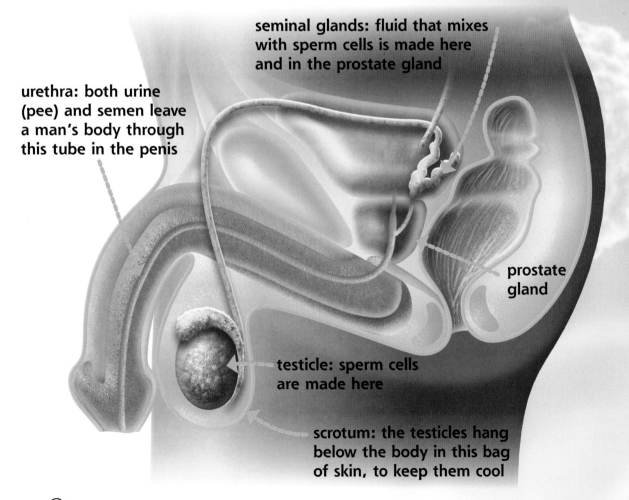

seminal glands: fluid that mixes with sperm cells is made here and in the prostate gland

urethra: both urine (pee) and semen leave a man's body through this tube in the penis

prostate gland

testicle: sperm cells are made here

scrotum: the testicles hang below the body in this bag of skin, to keep them cool

⚲ **A boy's reproductive organs grow during puberty, and start to do new things.**

How else do hormones affect my body?

Hormones can play havoc with your skin, causing spots and a new type of sweat. The good news is that these changes won't last forever.

Boys and girls often get spots, or pimples, during **puberty**. Changing hormones around the time of a girl's period can also cause spots.

Hormones make skin oilier than normal. The oil traps bacteria in the tiny holes that cover your skin. As your body fights the bacteria, pus builds up. Pus is a mixture of bacteria and old, damaged **cells** which can cause red, sore, swollen spots. An outbreak of lots of spots is called acne.

SCIENCE BEHIND THE MYTH

MYTH: People get spots by eating fatty foods.

SCIENCE: Hormones are to blame for spots, not fatty foods! However, eating a healthy diet, drinking plenty of water, and washing your skin gently can help to keep spots under control.

Smelly sweat

Hormones even change the way your skin sweats. Sweat glands under your armpits and between your legs start to make a thick, waxy substance that bacteria live in and feed on. The bacteria release smelly chemicals that cause body odour (B.O.).

Showering or bathing daily, using an anti-perspirant deodorant, and changing out of damp clothes after exercise will keep body odour under control. You don't need to start using lots of perfumed sprays, as these can clog up your skin even more.

🔍 **Many boys and girls start to use deodorant during puberty.**

How will I feel when puberty starts?

Hormones don't just cause physical changes, they also affect your emotions. During **puberty** you can feel amazing one day and sad the next, for no particular reason.

Practical advice

Who can I talk to about my worries?

It can help to talk about how you're feeling. Parents, carers, teachers, school nurses, and doctors have all gone through puberty themselves and can answer your questions. Your doctor or nurse can also give you practical advice, like information about sanitary towels and tampons. If you'd rather speak to someone you don't know, you could contact an organization such as Childline.

Maybe you are best friends with your parents over the weekend, but feel embarrassed when they collect you from school. You might feel angry when adults seem to treat you like a child. Many girls also have mini mood swings just before their period starts each month.

Treat yourself

These emotions are confusing. The best way to cope is to be your own best friend. Treating yourself can help you to feel happier. Perhaps you could take a relaxing bath, or take time out to read a book or watch a film. You could also try going for a walk or playing a sport. Exercise releases "happy" chemicals, giving you more energy and improving your mood.

Some people find it helpful to keep a diary. You can write your worries down, and remind yourself of all the good things in life.

What is the best way to cope with puberty?

Your body goes through amazing changes during **puberty**. Over a few years, you'll gain a fifth of your adult height and half of your adult weight. Girls will grow breasts and start having periods. Boys will grow facial hair and start producing sperm. These things are a normal part of growing up.

🔍 **Puberty changes can take place quickly or slowly. This means that your friends may be at a very different stage. But you will all develop in the same way in the end.**

It's normal to worry about how you look – after all, your body has not changed so quickly since you were a baby.

At some point everyone gets worried about the way his or her body is changing. It can be very difficult if you are the first one in your class to get body hair, or the last to get your period.

Remember that everyone goes through puberty – even celebrities. Film posters, magazines, and television programmes use all sorts of tricks to make their stars look perfect. Underneath, you can be sure that they are experiencing some of the same worries as you.

Your amazing body

Puberty hormones target many different areas of your body. They bring about the changes that help boys grow into men and girls into women. Look at these pictures to find out some of the changes you will experience.

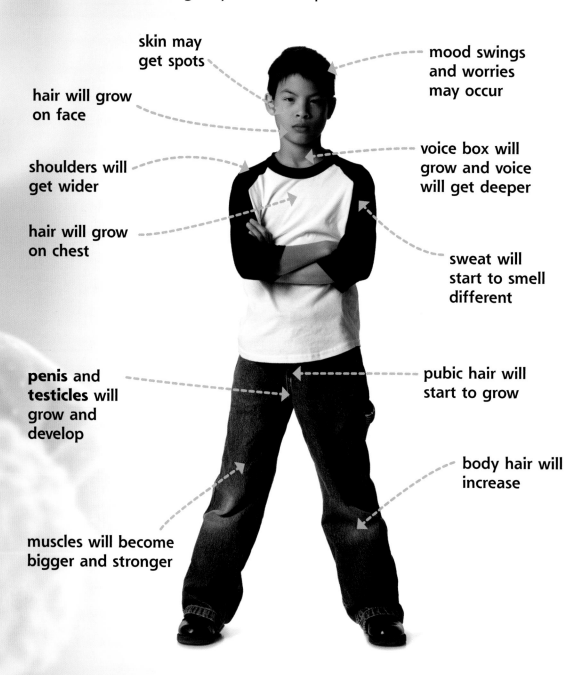

skin may get spots

mood swings and worries may occur

hair will grow on face

voice box will grow and voice will get deeper

shoulders will get wider

hair will grow on chest

sweat will start to smell different

penis and **testicles** will grow and develop

pubic hair will start to grow

body hair will increase

muscles will become bigger and stronger

Your body is programmed to change in these ways. You can't do anything to stop or speed up puberty. Each boy and girl will develop at a time that is right for his or her body.

skin may get spots

mood swings and worries may occur

sweat will start to smell different

breasts will start to grow

body will become curvier

ovaries will start releasing an egg once every month

hips will get wider

pubic hair will start to grow

periods will start

body hair will increase

Glossary

cell smallest part of a living thing

cycle series of events that happen over and over again

egg cell special cell released by a woman's ovaries. Egg cells are needed for reproduction.

fertilize when one sperm cell joins with one egg cell and starts to grow into a baby

growth spurt when weight and height increase very quickly

hormones chemical messengers that cause changes in the body

mature grow and develop into adult form

menstrual cycle cycle that prepares a woman's body for pregnancy and causes her to have periods

ovaries pair of organs in a girl's body that mature during puberty and begin to release egg cells

penis part of a boy's body that matures during puberty. Both urine and sperm leave the body through the penis.

puberty time when a child's body develops and matures into an adult's body, able to reproduce

reproduction process by which living things make new individuals

sperm cell special cell made by a man's testicles. Sperm cells are needed for reproduction.

testicles pair of organs in a boy's body that mature during puberty and begin to make sperm cells

uterus (also called a womb) organ in a girl's body that develops and matures during puberty, ready to carry a growing baby when the girl is an adult

vagina passage linking a girl's uterus to the outside of her body

Find out more

Books

Facts of Life: What's Happening to Me? (Girls), Susan Meredith (Usborne, 2006)

Girls Only! All about Periods and Growing-up Stuff, Vic Parker (Hodder Children's Books, 2004)

The Period Book: Everything You Don't Want to Ask (But Need to Know), Karen and Jennifer Gravelle (Piatkus Books, 1997)

Websites and Organizations

www.childrenfirst.nhs.uk/teens/life/puberty_body_tour/ index.html

Visit this NHS website to take a puberty body tour and find out what's going on inside your body and mind.

www.nhs.uk/Livewell/puberty/Pages/pubertyhome.aspx

Watch a video of children and teenagers talking about their experiences of growing up and the changes in their bodies. A doctor also explains what happens during puberty.

www.childline.org.uk

Telephone: 0800 1111

Whatever your worries, people at Childline are there to listen and to help. You can even get advice and information by text message.

Index